Spiritual Rain for the Dry Soul

Jennifer D. Murphy

Destiny House Publishing, LLC.

P.O. Box 19774

Detroit, MI 48219

www.destinyhousepublishing.com

inquiry@destinyhousepublishing.com

888.890.9455

Artwork: Pexels.com

ISBN-13:
978-1936867431

ISBN-10:
1936867435

DEDICATION

I dedicate this book to the awesome man that God has given me, Dedrick O. Murphy, Sr. He, through much sacrifice, has given to me unselfishly. Thank you for the support and the endless nights that you held me in your arms. You've seen the good, the bad, and the ugly and you still loved me. Thank you so much for being my gift. You are an amazing man and I have never known a love like this. This one is for you.

You have changed my life in so many ways
You've taken me from darkness to light and turned my midnights into days

With you I feel like I can do anything but fail
Holding tight to your hand and allowing our love to be strong and prevail

Your love has brought out the best in me
Allowing my heart to feel endless emotion and finally be set free

Dedrick, my love, only you have captivated my heart
in more ways than one
I feel like our lives have been made complete and we
have just begun

You've given me love in a way that I've never known
A heart of love, understanding, and faithfulness you
have shown

When God created you, he knew just what to do
For out of your body, He molded me to love you

For he has given a very special gift to me
To cherish from now until eternity

That gift is no secret, or great mystery
We've been given each other to reach our destiny

So as I take my gift and hold it close to my heart
I pray that the love it brings, will continue to impart

Great blessings and add no sorrow
For my gift from God has brought me hope for
tomorrow

My endless love, Dedrick O. Murphy Sr.

CONTENTS

Page

ACKNOWLEDGMENTS

I would first like to thank God for the vision and for trusting me enough with the words of his heart. He has never and will never let me down. To my parents, Archie and Joyce Shurn thanks for being the awesome people of God that you are, and for being a constant reflection of God's glory. I am grateful for all that you've placed inside of me from birth up until now. Keep pressing up the King's highway. I would like to thank leaders who impacted my Christian journey (Pastor Samuel and Mother Ruth Diggins, Apostle DK and Prophetess Alice Jones, and Pastor Ric and Sue Thomas). A special thanks to my spiritual parents, Bishop Edgar Allen and the late Mother Enyess Allen, your wealth of knowledge and wisdom has been an incredible foundation and I could never repay you for what you've imparted. Thank you for believing in what God placed in me and for the endless support you provided Dedrick and myself. To my Pastors, Kim and Steve Outlaw, thank you for being a guiding light and a breath of fresh air when I needed it the most. Your commitment to serve and pray for me and my family has catapulted us to a whole new dimension. Doing life with you has strengthened us beyond our imagination. We love you both so very much. Thank you for birthing Living Water Fellowship Church.   To my prayer partners, warriors, and sisters in Christ, thank you so much for the friendship and the bond we share, and of course the countless powerful prayer sessions. Our love is indestructible. To my 9 brothers and sisters for pushing me to my wits end with worry, anger, laughter, joy, and tears. I love each of you and pray God's blessing upon you. May you find your way through Christ. To my nieces and nephews, may you grow up to be awesome leaders and powerful instruments to be used by God, line up with His will and move into your destiny. To all of the young ladies that I've had the opportunity to mentor, teach, love, and encourage thank you for trusting me through the rough moments of your life and for pulling me up in the spirit when I thought that I had nothing left to give. You have truly been my lifeline. To my seeds, (Haley, Hannah and Dedrick Jr. and my unborn) all of you are gifts to your parents and to this world, live life to the fullest and never give up. You will bless many with the gifts that are within you. Your very presence is a gift! To my coworkers at MCPHD thanks for making me laugh when things got rough. We had the best lunchtime fun. To my Kentucky State University family, thanks for all the countless precious memories and moments of personal growth. Our bond is endless #soThoro, #KSUproud. Thanks to all my friends and family that supported the vision of this book, your kindness has made my dream a reality and I will never forget you. To my husband, the true wind beneath my wings. Thank you for always believing in me. I dedicate this first one to you.

1
INTRODUCTION

Often times in a world full of gloom and doom, it's hard to imagine yourself at peace. It's also hard to keep a smile on your face when everything around you appears to be crumbling. That is why it is so necessary for us to refresh our body, mind, and soul. We do this by taking time out and allowing God to drench us with his rain. That's right, spiritual rain.

What is spiritual rain? How can I get it? Let me tell you how you can have direct access to a well that will never run dry. In these pages, my hope is that you will find yourself drifting into a place of intrigue. During the writing of this book, I totally lost myself. I have compiled every experience both sad and joyous as I traveled down the road to my ultimate destination of deliverance. Hold onto your seats because this will be a ride that you will enjoy and ultimately feel refreshed with a new determination to live life as if tomorrow doesn't exist.

On this journey called life, there are many mysteries, some you may have to dig for and others lie right before your face; but only become clearer as you live. My deepest passion was to find what God had for me to do. I wanted to know where I fit in His equation of "Thy Kingdom Come". What was my role in the whole earthly realm? Then one day, I started writing, and my passion was revealed by the very words I placed on the page. My gift was awakened as I poured my heart through an ink pen and a small paperback journal.

Each day, I would meet God and I would write to him, expressing the matters of my heart and mind. Then, one day as I quieted myself, he began to speak back and the words that he spoke pushed me into my destiny and simply changed my life. He spoke words that pierced my very being. I could feel his presence lingering throughout the room where I sat. And this was the beginning of "Spiritual Rain for my Dry Soul" it was a time of refreshing and I never wanted to leave, and I knew I didn't have to. The good thing about God is that when you speak to Him and are still, he will begin speaking right back to you. I was once asked "How do you know when God is talking?" Well, I answered "God will come to you in a familiar voice "My sheep hear my voice, and I know them, and they follow me" John 10:27. It's an inner voice that prompts you to do well, that's God speaking. It made so much sense to me that I would never be alone again. When I found myself in a place where I didn't know what to do; I would go to that place with my pen and journal in hand and I would find refuge in the words that flowed from his heart to mine. This is the essence of Spiritual Rain for the Dry Soul.

Some of the chapters will include direct entries from my personal journal or just my exceptional experiences with the Father. Enjoy as you dive into a sea of infinite possibilities and swim the endless canals of hope. This will truly be a new beginning for you as you experience the well that will never run dry, His name Is Jesus! Use this time alone in God's presence to refuel your fire, or to get burning....burning with a passion to experience God on a whole new level.

"Rain to me signifies the outpouring of the Holy Ghost and, I ask you Lord to drench me!" JDM

TAKE THIS TIME TO WRITE DOWN AREAS THAT YOU HAVE

STRUGGLED, AND THEN PRAY THAT GOD OPEN YOUR HEART TO RECEIVE ALL THAT HE HAS FOR YOU AS YOU RELEASE THESE STRUGGLES TO HIM.

NOTES

_____

_____

_____

_____

_____

_____

_____

_____

_____

_____

_____

_____

_____

_____

_____

_____

_____

_____

_____

_____

_____

2

LET THE RAIN BEGIN TO FALL

Deep within my heart I feel a sudden drought. No longer do I have a sense of security in my being. I have drifted to a land less traveled by man where there is no longer greenery, only dry desert and sand. My soul needs relief in this dry and empty place. What was once a blossoming flower has now become an empty vase. Scattered pieces of my heart lie hopelessly on the ground, longing one day soon to be found. Nowhere to run and nowhere to hide, I look to the hills for strength and as a spiritual guide.

As I fall face first into the sand, I suddenly feel a lifting of my hands. The sky began to darken and mumble strong words, words of restoration, renewal, and reward. It sounded like the heavens were calling my name, I felt the earth shake beneath me and I knew in that moment that my situation was about to change. Then a great mist swept through the air and I slowly started to rise feeling a lifting of my cares. I beheld the beauty of what was falling from the sky, my sight became clearer as I wiped my eyes. It was God's hands opening up and something coming out. When I took another glance, I knew it was my chance, to put an end to this emotional slow dance. I could lift up my head and never look back, gaining strength from my journey through the things that I lacked. When God chooses you and sets you apart, he wants to add an awesome finish to what He starts.

So with humility I allow you to take full control...now I can receive spiritual rain for my dry soul.

"Those who consistently hunger and thirst after righteousness shall be filled."

Scripture reference Matthew 5:6

A Moment to Pray

Lord, as I began to read the words of these pages I pray that you open up my heart to receive spiritual rain. I know that you have more for me and I want this book to propel me into my destiny. God, I am emptying myself so that I can receive from you all that you have for me. Here I am, Lord. Here I am.

Have your way in me. Rain Jesus, Reign. In Jesus Name. Amen.

Notes

_____

_____

_____

_____

_____

_____

_____

_____

_____

_____

_____

_____

_____

_____

_____

_____

_____

_____

_____

_____

_____

_____

_____

_____

_____

_____

_____

_____

_____

_____

_____

_____

_____

_____

_____

_____

_____

_____

_____

_____

_____

_____

_____

_____

_____

_____

_____

_____

_____

_____

3
VALUING YOU: CHECK YOUR TAG

This is dedicated to the young single women and the young at heart, everywhere. Many times, we forget; or maybe some of us never discovered our own value.   We are each unique and valuable and precious in the sight of God.   For the next 10-15 minutes, I want you to think about yourself and how you see yourself right now in this moment. Then, use the blank pages to write down your thoughts using one-word descriptions (i.e. afraid, fearless, bold, etc.) and be honest (2mins).

_____

_____

_____

_____

_____

_____

_____

_____

_____

_____

_____

_____

_____

_____

_____

Scriptures to read:

Gen 1:27
Proverbs 31:10
Ephesians 2:20
Proverbs 31:26
Song of Solomon 4:7
Ps 34:5

The Marion Webster dictionary describes virtue as a good or admirable quality; excellence, goodness, and righteousness. When God created us, he placed inside of us great treasures. Colossians 2:1-6

The woman was made to touch God very differently than the man. The woman, as complicated as she may be, is full of so much compassion, drive, and determination.

Let me ask you a couple of questions:

Can you walk into a jewelry store and pick up a diamond without asking permission to see it from the owner or the one in charge? Have you ever been to a fragrance counter and purchased a tester bottle of cologne?   Or when you are ready to purchase do they give you the one behind the locked glass counter that has not been touched?

I ask those questions to show you that when something is valuable it cannot be handled by just anyone. There should be a price on you that is so high, that only the one that God meant for you to have and be connected with would be willing to pay the price.

That means God does not put anything on sale, so you shouldn't either. He does not do markdowns or price cuts.   You must realize how God sees you. Proverbs 31:10 talks about the value of a virtuous woman and how her price is higher than rubies. If you have discounted yourself, so that you can hang around people who don't believe what you believe, or do things that you know in your heart are wrong I am challenging you to <u>check your tag</u>. There should be so many zeroes following whatever number you see.

23

Friends that come into your life should not cause you to compromise your morals. If they do, you need to get some new ones. A lot of times you may think, I can change them. And I am not saying that it's wrong to think that way, but if you find them changing you, more than you are changing them, then you need to reevaluate your friendships.

You must see yourself through the eyes of the One who created you…and what He sees when He looks at you should be a reflection of himself! When something is mishandled it appears to be damaged and that's what happens to us when we don't value ourselves. We allow others to mishandle us. I was once told "people will only treat you how you allow them to". As I live, I have found this to be undeniably true. Don't fear or worry. God is definitely able to restore you to your naturally, beautiful state; but you must be willing to go through the process.

The true measure of a woman is valued by the glory that is revealed and shown through her. It is the brightness of her light. Don't give up on the promises of God. Hold out until God sends the right one your way. I am a living witness that when the right one comes nothing else will matter. I have experienced extreme devastation by allowing my heart to be intertwined with people who were not my perfect match. Yes, God does want us to fellowship and have a good time; but in a pure and holy way. When I realized my value through constant communion with God, he delivered me and I became an ex-tester (remember the perfume counter).

Everyone you meet is not your husband. You may be sent a friend to mature you, challenge you into greater, and more. You must line yourself up with God so that your vision is not obscured when the right one comes your way. I was always told that if your hands are full of the wrong thing, don't expect God to deliver the right thing, because there is no room. God will grant you so much favor when you are walking in his light, not only that but he will even give you choices. Now, that's when you know he loves you. Remember how valuable you are and how someone must be willing to pay the price to be in your circle. Don't waste yourself on things or people that discredit the person God made you to be. There is nothing worth having your character discounted. So please, check your tag!

A Moment to Pray

Lord, as you are revealing yourself to me, open my ears, heart, and eyes. I know that you have made me just the way you desire me to be. Unfortunately, I don't always like what I see. But God, I thank you for the value you've placed inside of me. Help me not to take myself for granted, nor allow others to discount my value. I am precious to you and I will not compromise who I am to fit in with the world's idea of perfection. I am fearfully and wonderfully made in your image and I know that you have so much in store for me. My value is far above rubies, and I know that you are restoring me to my God ordained state. Thank you for helping me to check my tag and realize how priceless I really am. In Jesus Name. Amen.

Notes

_____

_____

_____

_____

_____

_____

_____

4
RIDING THROUGH THE STORM

One day as I was taking a trip to visit my hometown in South Bend IN, the rain began to pour. Now, at this time in my life, I didn't have a lot of experience driving in severe storms.

Needless to say when the rain began to fall, I felt the urge to panic. I thought to myself, "Should I pull over at a gas station until the rain stops or off on the shoulder of the road?" I remembered my husband (we were just dating then) told me never to pull over on the shoulder because large trucks and other vehicles would not be able to see me during heavy rain. With his words in mind, I continued driving and I became more and more afraid.

Suddenly, I heard the Lord say "Pray". As I began to pray I started to feel a sense of relief, the rain was not becoming lighter, but God had begun to send peace. As I relaxed myself, I tuned into what I felt God was leading me into (a precious moment with him). I heard him say "Daughter, keep driving" I said, "Lord are you sure?" He replied, "Keep driving." I asked, "Why?" He said, "As long as you are moving through the storm, you will come out. You cannot remain stagnant or pull over to the side because you will never get to the other side; or when you get to the other side after delaying you may miss out on what I have in store for you." Of course now the light bulb was turning on and I was so grateful for the revelation. God was not saying that the storm wouldn't come, but when it does come, know that your hope lies on the other side. Don't stay in the storm. If you keep moving, the storm will be over much sooner.

We move through our storms by the word and faith. Of course, as God poured these words out from his heart, I began to cry and realized that trouble doesn't last always. That was another awesome moment with the Father. He taught me a very valuable lifelong lesson. Remember, even through the storm, God is making something out of nothing. Through every storm, know that he is molding, cleansing, and conforming you to his will. When you go through storms, it may be to strip you bare or cleanse you in a way that is necessary for growth. Just ask God to help you endure the storm so that you can began to grow and flourish in his service and come out on the other side.

A Moment to Pray

Lord, the storms of life have taken me into some really dark places, some I didn't believe I would recover. I thank you now that you never leave me nor forsake me. I know that the storms of life will come and go. I want you to know that I will keep moving no matter what. At times my situation appears very tough, but I know with you, I can make it. Thank you for being my strength and my source of help in the time of trouble. If it were not for the storm, I would not be where I am today. Thank you because I have a better understanding of what to do in a storm and that's to keep on moving. No weapon formed against me will be able to prosper and I will rise to the occasion. I appreciate your patience and love for me and I will remain connected to you as I ride out every storm. In Jesus Name. Amen.

Notes

_____

_____

_____

_____

_____

_____

_____

_____

_____

_____

_____

_____

_____

_____

_____

_____

_____

_____

_____

_____

_____

_____

_____

_____

_____

_____

5
WEARING A MASK: WILL THE REAL YOU PLEASE STAND UP?

Many of us have gone throughout our lives putting on and taking off our different masks. We mask our frustrations, hurts, disappointments, failures and sometimes our success, for fear of people looking at us a certain way. Why do we cover what we are feeling? Or who we are? When God designed you (Jeremiah. 1:5) He knew exactly what He would put inside of you both in the beginning and as you live out your days. You were not put on this earth to hide who you are; but to fulfill your divine purpose. You are unique, and it doesn't matter if you don't fit the "cookie cutter" image that the world tries to paint as perfect. You are the only you and you cannot be duplicated. Did you know that there are gifts inside of you that are specifically designed to bring life? Not only to you but those individuals that need what you have (I Corinthians 4:7). It should be your goal to find out what your divine purpose is or where your inner treasure lies while you are here. Maybe it's to be a mother and supply your child or children with the best support and nurturing around. Maybe it's to empower other women to overcome abusive relationships and situations, or a father to instill awesome character in your sons and daughters. It may be to invent something that will change our everyday lives forever. Whatever your purpose is, ask God to make it real to you. Our mask keeps us from fulfilling God's plan. We suppress unhealed hurts, unmet needs, and unfulfilled desires and these often become the source of our illnesses and setbacks (Pastor Donald Clark, Chicago Illinois). We allow others to insult our character and keep us from moving forward.

Satan knows that if he can distract you long enough by changing your focus off of the things that matter most to you, he will have you. He knows that if you take your mask off and reveal who God made you to be, then his territory would be in danger of defeat. Today is a new day, one filled with awesome possibilities. You can have what you desire. Jesus said, "No good thing will I withhold from them that love me who walk upright before me." Psalms 84:1.

God's desire is for you to prosper he says, "Beloved, I wish above all things that you would prosper and be in good health even as your soul prospers" III John 1:2. So, take a moment and look deep within your heart and ask yourself what is my burning desire? If I could live one day in my purpose what would I be doing? What would I be wearing? Who would I meet? How would I feel? After you answer those questions close your eyes and visualize each of those answers. Go ahead close them. Now that you've seen it, move toward it! The enemy thought you would never see it, but guess what? You just did, he is already defeated. Take charge of your life and make decisions that will move you forward. Follow those dreams you've always had and know that it's not too late. It may take a lot of time and energy, but the payoff will be tremendous. I challenge you to possess the land (Deuteronomy 1:8). Pull off your mask and put your best face forward. Will the real you please stand up?

"The enemy usually fights those who know who they are, and whose they are. Take flight and never look back." JM

A Moment to Pray

Lord, awaken my senses and allow me to rise to the occasion that you are calling me to fulfill. I am courageous and bold in you, and I can do anything but fail as long as you are my guide. This is a new beginning and I am taking off the many masks that have kept me hidden. I want the world to see the awesome person you have created. Thank you for releasing a sense of security and Godly pride within my spirit now. I am on my way to greatness, and I will not be held back by fear, doubt, shame, or lack of knowledge. I will possess the land that you set aside for me. I will leap over barriers and tear down walls. Thank you for a new day and enabling me to take flight. I will live life completely and fully. In Jesus Name. Amen.

Notes

_____

_____

_____

_____

_____

_____

_____

_____

_____

6

STRONGHOLDS OF SEXUAL SIN

I am not an expert by any means. But I know from my life experiences how sexual sin can keep you bound in a world of confusion, delusion, and ultimate destruction.

As a young lady growing up, I had many things that I desired to do. I had dreams, and wanted to accomplish big things; but those things began to change when I became entangled in a life of sexual sin. My desire to chase after my goals became less appealing and I became very lazy.

First, I would like to say that I was not what the older folks would say "loose" but I was on a road to becoming just that. I had found pleasure in the things that my flesh liked and I wanted them more and more. Now, you may be saying "that will not happen to me" or some may be saying "that's the same thing that happened to me". Whatever your statement is, know that you are not alone. Many of us have said, "Maybe, I will just try it once" and once was all it took to get hooked, and into the place you are now in or was once delivered from.

Sexual sins have a way of enticing you and carrying you to a place that seems like no return. Once you try one thing, you either want to do it again or try something else to see if it gets better. The one thing I know for sure is that outside of the marriage covenant, sex ruins your emotions and will have you seeing double for a while.

The Bible says that a "double-minded man is unstable in all his ways" James 1:8. This is so true; I found it hard to make decisions, concentrating, and even focusing on the small things that were going on in my life. I was an emotional wreck, and it only got worse the more I engaged in sexual sin. When you open yourself up to a man or woman who is not your lifetime partner through the covenant of marriage, you open yourself up to receive every part of that individual. So, the issues he or she has often become your issues.

Have you ever heard the phrase, "soul ties"? Well, your souls become literally tied together when you have intercourse. If you are not the first woman/man that the man/woman has been with, every tie that is connected to him, gets connected to you and that's how you become entangled.

There are many strings intertwined creating a web of deceit and strong bondage. The woman being the receptacle and the man being the projector, everything that is inside of him gets dumped into you. Have you ever felt like garbage? Well, if you've had sex outside of marriage it's probably because of this very thing. The man after reaching his climatic state projects all that is inside of him into you. It sounds dramatic, but it's true. You become the dumping ground for that man. I'm not calling you garbage but hopefully you are feeling the urge to read on and bring closure to whatever your sexual struggle has been.

Let's get back to the message. Sexual sin leaves you in a place of vulnerability, and as I stated before, delusion. Have you ever had those playbacks in your mind that make it seem like the experience was so dramatically long and exotic? But you know it was only a few minutes. Well, that is what the enemy will do to bring your mind back to that place so that you will do it again and again. A few moments of fleshly pleasure can leave you in several weeks, months, or even years of spiritual deficiency. Why do we keep going back? I believe that whatever you feed will always be the strongest. So, if you feed the flesh with the things it likes, it ultimately gains strength.

On the other hand, if you feed your spirit more, it will be the one that gains the upper hand. You cannot expect your spirit to rise up when you are in those tempting places because you have not done anything to support that reaction. You must be willing to put in the time through prayer, reading the word, and spending time with positive people that will challenge you and hold you accountable. These are the things that will strengthen your spirit. You must also be willing to cut sin off at the source, that means starve the flesh. If you have been living in sexual sin for a while, you pretty much know what entices you. That is where the challenge lies; you must be ready to address the very root or the initial onset in order to break free from the constant struggle.

There are many forms of sexual sin (i.e. fornication, adultery, pornography, masturbation, same sex relationships, and many others). Whatever your struggle is, God is able to help you overcome it. It will not be easy, and whatever you do to get free, you must continue to do it to remain free. Many times after we are delivered we become comfortable and decrease our efforts when seeking God. We cannot do that, you must be totally committed to your deliverance and nurture it each day.

Your desire to be free must outweigh everything including personal gratification. Like the older folks use to say, "You got to get sick and tired of being sick and tired." That is exactly what it will take to birth your deliverance and maintain it. God is only waiting on you. I don't have all the answers in this book but there are several godly resources available that specialize in each of the areas mentioned above, and nothing is too hard for God. Seek out those resources, not neglecting the word of God which has all the answers. (II Timothy 3:16 "All Scripture is God-breathed and is useful for teaching, rebuking, correcting and training in righteousness.")

Don't ever feel that you cannot go to him because of the sin in your life. The reason he died on the cross was for our sins so don't be ashamed to bring them to him. There are many people you know, family members, friends, pastors, and others in Christian leadership who have struggled with the same thing. What separates the "delivered" is that they constantly rely on God to keep them that way. Jesus is our help and we must not forget to call on him during the good and the bad times. God is a great deliverer and is able to help you destroy the works of the flesh. Yes, even those things you did that you couldn't tell anybody about, he can deliver.

The one thing that helped me when I struggled with sexual sin was not placing myself in situations that would compromise my desire to please God. This is really hard when you feel like you want to be with someone. It takes much discipline and a greater desire to please God instead of yourself or the other person.

My husband and I met in college and yes the emotions were very high. As we both matured in Christ and became engaged we had to make a total commitment to not even cuddle, the closer it got to the wedding, because we knew how much our bodies burned with passion down on the inside. If we touched, we would ignite an unquenchable fire. I am saying that to say, keep yourself from cozy corners and dark dorm rooms, because those places will always lead you down a path that may leave you "Coo Coo for Cocoa Puffs" if you know what I mean. In the covenant of marriage sex is a beautiful thing. It can be as awesome as you make it.

The Bible says in Hebrews 13:4, "Marriage is honorable and the bed undefiled" that means even in marriage we can defile the bed if we venture down the roads that lead us into sin. You may be saying, "What does that mean?" Well, if you and your spouse find pleasure in watching others have sex then you're inviting other spirits in and that could potentially lead to unlawful desires for someone else. Also, the idea of an "open marriage" is cancerous. The Bible is clear in Exodus 20:17 "Thou shalt not covet thy neighbor's wife". These exercises open your home up to several demonic spirits that can find a home in your children.

It's a very dangerous thing to play with God. I am not saying that you cannot be adventurous with toys, role-playing, and gadgets; enjoy, but realize that marital sex is about giving honor to God through the loving intimate touches of husband and wife. It's about serving one another at a deep an intimate level. Tell me, what would Jesus do?

A Moment to Pray (Singles)

Lord, I come to you now asking that you help me to be more like you. I ask that you hear me now and create in me a clean heart and place in me the "Do-Right" spirit. I know that I cannot live without your protection and your love. I need you to wash me and make me whole. Forgive me for all sexual sins past and present and come into my life and teach me how to live holy through your word. I know that you died for me and that you will soon return for those who choose to live for you. I have abused myself by entering into sexual sin. I am so sorry and I need you to help me. You are my only hope and I need you right now. Hear my cry and deliver me from sexual sin now.

Teach me the steps to draw nearer to you. I know as I draw nearer to you, the farther I will be from the sin that once controlled me. I don't want to be left behind. On this day, I make a commitment to serve you and keep you always on my mind. I will focus on spending more time to pray, read your word, and do those things that will strengthen my relationship with you. It's not about what church I go to but about having a sincere devotion and desire to please you. I pray this prayer with sincerity in Jesus Name Amen.

A Moment to Pray (Married Couples)

Lord, my husband and I want to bring honor to you. We don't want to defile our marriage, or the bed when coming together in sexual intimacy. Lord, we know that you gave us each other to share wonderful things, not to bring others in on it through television, videos, or in person. Lord, help us to bring honor to you at all times and forgive us for being so selfish. We pray that you intervene now and destroy those unlawful desires. The desires for another that make me aroused. I pray that _____ (husband or wife) be able to satisfy the needs of my flesh. Help us to communicate on a level that will increase our sexual energy for each other. Allow us to only look upon each other for that sheer satisfaction. Keep us from entering into ungodly soul ties. And those ties that were created before marriage let them be destroyed. You are able to cleanse us from all unrighteousness, and we welcome you in our hearts and home to do so. Let our sexual experiences together glorify you. Help us to serve one another in love and deed. God, we ask this in your mighty son, Jesus's Name.

Notes

_____

_____

_____

_____

_____

_____

_____

_____

_____

_____

_____

_____

_____

_____

_____

_____

_____

_____

_____

_____

_____

7
DIRECT ME O' GOD

Personal Reflection

Obstacles challenge my every move
Trying to stop great ideas and disable my groove
Distractions come to make me troubled to forget my
purpose and cause a huge struggle. Endless decisions
that I have to make, praying and waiting to see if my
life lines up with fate. Angered and often set adrift.
Only to realize that God's hand will always serve to
uplift. Concerned about what life will throw next
Convinced that whatever it is; it will only be a test.
Drowning in self-pity, oh what a shame! If I would
just call on His sweet and precious name. He came
to give me life and it more abundantly. If I would
just ask my heart, my mind, and my soul, would be
set free.

Okay, here it goes without any hesitation because I
know I have a divine destination. Jesus, Jesus, no

other help I know. For great is thy faithfulness, it always steals the show.

Humbly, I bow in your great presence to seek your face and give you reverence. Help me, O' God, I ask you today; let not my heart be troubled while you are showing me the way. Prove to me what is acceptable and true. Give me the desire of my heart that is to only serve You. Help me O' God in my times of distress, to constantly trust and continually press. Lord your word is strengthening and powerful too. Help me complete the work you've called me to do.

Notes

_____

_____

_____

_____

_____

_____

_____

_____

_____

_____

_____

_____

_____

_____

8
HOW THIRSTY ARE YOU?

Now, I would like to take you on a trip, one that will hopefully bring you to a place of self-evaluation. You will no longer look at others and their shortcomings but turn the focus on yourself: me, myself and I. It's very important that you begin to focus on "Who you are? Who you want to become? And what you should be doing?" The world continues to take a turn for the worst and unless you are totally convinced that you are living a life that is pleasing to God you must take a moment or two and work on self.

So as you read this, I want you to ask yourself "How will this help me to improve my walk with Christ?" This word, if you are reading it, was specifically designed for you. So, come and go with me.

Picture yourself in a desert, running. It's about 100 degrees and the sun is beaming down on your face. All you see is miles long of desert sand surrounded by cacti and tumbleweeds. There is not even a single breeze in the air, but you are running.

Sweat begins to pour off of your body and finally you stop to get a drink from your one and only water bottle. You tilt the bottle upward and nothing; the bottle is dry. The only reason you kept running was because you knew that when you finished you would be able to drink. Your eyes fill up with tears because you see no way out. You look around and see no one else. By this time you find it very difficult to swallow because your throat is just that dry?

What will you do now? There is no sign of relief anywhere. You feel so hopeless when suddenly out of nowhere the sky begins to release drops of rain.

Do you tilt your head back and open your mouth wide; do you cup your hands and try to catch enough water to drink for that moment? Do you take the lid off of your water bottle and wait until the bottle fills up? What do you do? How long will this rain last?

How thirsty are you? As you think of each possible solution to your problem of thirst think of this, if you knew the rain would only last 1 minute, would your choice be different?

Would you waste time thinking about what your next move would be?

Would you try other solutions before the obvious solution?

Would you sit on the ground pouting, complaining and eventually give up missing out on all the opportunities?

Or would you take every opportunity to catch enough water that would last a long time?

What would you do? How thirsty are you?

Well, let's take a deeper look into this scenario and hear what God is saying. Many times, we, as Christians or people of God, can become so dry as if we have been running for days without water. We neglect to take the opportunity to drink from the well that God has so freely given us. In John 6:35 (NIV) Jesus replied, "I am the bread of life. Whoever comes to me will never be hungry again. Whoever believes in me will never be thirsty." That means that when you become a believer through the acceptance of

Jesus Christ into your heart and true turning away from sin, you gain access to what the Bible is saying. The Bible also states in Matthew 5: 6 "Blessed are those who hunger and thirst after righteousness for they shall be filled."

We go throughout life doing our own thing, wasting time, as if the rain of God's forgiveness, goodness, mercy, grace, favor, protection, and love will never cease to exist. We feel like "Once I get myself together then I will serve God, with my whole heart" If you could get yourself together, God would not have sent his only born son to die on a cross for you. He knew what this world would become and because of the love that he has for you, he paid the price on cavalry. After all of that, we are still worried about the "little things", falling out with loved ones over the "little things", losing sleep over the "little things" missing out on God and his greatness over the "little things". How thirsty are you?

Well, I am writing this book to tell you that it's not too late to begin drinking from the well that will never run dry. In John 7:37 "On the last day, the climax of the festival, Jesus stood and shouted to the crowds, anyone who is thirsty may come to me!"

You will see that the well that God provides will satisfy your deepest yearning and it's plentiful. David wrote in Psalms 63:1 "O'God thou art my God, early will I seek thee: my soul thirsteth for thee in a dry and thirsty land, where no water is." David is crying out in sincere desperation. See, we must become so thirsty for the Lord, his presence, and his kingdom to come here on earth.

We must ask the Lord and his spirit to enter our hearts and quench whatever deep thirst we may have. When you open yourself to receive God's spirit then you give him access to work on your behalf. The problem is that many of us are making decisions in a thirsty or "dry state". When you don't have the guidance of the Holy Ghost you remain in a dangerous place that could cause you to drink from other things (i.e. wrong relationships, alcohol, drugs, pornography, fornication, adultery, slander, lying, discontentment, and other demonically influenced activity). These things will only keep you enslaved in a vicious cycle.

"But the Comforter, which is the Holy Ghost, whom the Father will send in my name, he shall teach you all things, and bring all things to your remembrance, whatsoever I have said unto you." John 14:26

The only thing that will truly quench your thirst and break the cycle of sin in your life is confession, true repentance, and the in filling of the Holy Ghost. True repentance comes when you confess with your mouth and believe in your heart. "Believe in your heart", means that you are opening yourself up to change from your will to God's will. When you believe something you normally do all that you can to stand by what you believe in, and that is what God requires. Once you've confessed and repented meaning "turn-away" from a lifestyle that is not pleasing in the sight of God then you are ready to be filled with the Holy Ghost. The Holy Spirit is not a bunch of shouting, falling out, and tongues although it can be expressed in those ways. The true representation of being filled is a lifestyle that bears good fruit and the ability or power to make positive choices. The Holy Spirit cannot dwell in a vessel that is not pure. So it is important that you ask God, as David did in Psalms 90, "Create in me a clean heart oh God and renew the right spirit within me". If you truly want God to quench your thirst you must be willing to seek him daily and be sincere in your attitude and most importantly your heart when you come before him.

Sin destroys both life and fullness of the Holy Spirit within the believer. In John 3:8-9, John emphasizes that one who is truly born of God cannot make sin his/her way of life. Because the life of God cannot exist in one who "practices" sin or continues in sin. Only those who continue to abide in God (meaning putting away works of darkness) continue to be born of him. When you are thirsty, depression gets a hold to you and it does not want to let you go. You fall back into sin and then it becomes a never ending cycle. When you are thirsty, the enemy knows and he will begin to play on those things he knows you like. He knows that if he can distract and arouse you once again, you will fall back into sin, resulting in a delay of your God-given purpose. Did you know that when the devil is cast out of you and you return back into sin, you make his force stronger? In Matt 12:43-45 "When the unclean spirit is gone out of a man, he walketh through dry places, seeking rest, and findeth none. Then he saith, I will return into my house from whence I came out; and when he is come, he findeth it empty, swept, and garnished. Then goeth he, and taketh with himself seven other spirits more wicked than himself, and they enter in and dwell there: and the last state of that man is worse than the first. Even so shall it be also unto this wicked generation." That is why once you return to that sin, it becomes so much harder to let go; even when you are tired of doing it you cannot stop because the demonic force has become that much stronger. You may be sitting there reading this now and have become worried. But didn't I say we serve a merciful and loving God? He is able to fill you with a gift that will destroy every demonic attack and even uproot anything that keeps you entangled in that vicious cycle.

Are you tired of going to church for an emotional touch and going back to the same lifestyle? Do you want to spend the majority of your days searching for things that will not satisfy? Do you desire to feel God's hand at all times upon your life? Do you want the rivers of living waters to come alive within you? In John 7:38 the analogy of the rivers represents the gifts of the spirit that are locked inside the believers. When those rivers are activated, it allows the believers rivers to flow out and touch others with the message of Jesus Christ. Those rivers represent gifts, talents, and total greatness!

Take a stand to make a difference in your life today. Once you take a stand, then God is able to assist you in initiating change in others. That is how the gospel is spread. Are you willing to give up the past, I mean really give up those things that leave you empty? How thirsty are you? David said in Psalms 42:2 "My soul thirsteth for God, for the living God." Let's allow God to quench our thirsting souls and fill our spiritual cups until they overflow. How thirsty are you?

"Those who consistently hunger and thirst after righteousness shall be filled." (Matt 5:6)

A Moment to Pray

Lord, examine my heart and bring conviction if there are things that are not like you within me. Allow this word to penetrate and take root in my heart and bring forth change. I don't want to wander around this world in a thirsty state, but I want to drink from your well that will never run dry. I want to be able to make decisions that lead me into joy, peace, love, prosperity, and more fruitfulness. Forgive me, if I've been disobedient. I want to fulfill your calling upon my life. I speak against procrastination, fear, doubt, worry, and anxiety and I ask you to release a spirit of hope, obedience, and a new determination into my life. In Jesus Name. Amen.

Notes

_____

_____

_____

_____

_____

_____

_____

_____

_____

_____

_____

_____

_____

_____

_____

_____

_____

_____

_____

_____

_____

_____

9

BREAK ME TO RECEIVE THE RAIN

Being broken before the Lord is not always easy. It takes a lot of humility and willingness to lay it all out on the table, even though he knows everything. When you do this, it causes you to expose and be exposed. I'm not talking about running around town gossiping about what someone did to you etc. But I am referring to exposing the truth and root of an issue. When we ask God to put us in his will it often times involves uncovering, pain, and discomfort. The other side of that, as you continue to yield to him, you will experience joy, peace, endless love, and a new determination. God delights in an individual who is broken and contrite. The Bible says in Psalms 51:17 "A broken and contrite spirit is his delight" which means one that is sincere in their efforts of total submission has God's stamp of approval.

We all should desire that we be broken enough to receive all that God has for us. When God sees the intent of your heart and the purity of your spirit he will began to move quickly concerning all the things you petition. Many times, God's delays are to mature us and bring us to our expected destination. The scripture "to whom much is given, much is required" Luke 12:48, means in order to get all that God has for you, he is going to apply some pressure to different areas of your life to see if you can handle it. The more you can handle, the more he will give you.

I would see people and wonder "how did they get all of that, or why do they always get so much and I am still waiting?" Well, God simply answered me saying, "When I can trust you enough, I will give you the desires of your heart." That was a wake-up call and not something I really wanted to hear from my Father. But as I stated before, humility is a gift and it does not always feel good. In order to get to the place in God where there are no limits and you are able to move heaven, there is much sacrifice of time, resources, and energy; but the payoff is incredible.

Press on and keep allowing him to break you, the good news is that you will not regret it. Romans 8:18 say, "For the sufferings of this present time are not worthy to be compared to the glory that shall be revealed in us". Let him continue to do what he's doing and thank him all the way.

A Moment to Pray

Dear Lord, I come to you asking that you humble me. Humble my mind and my heart to receive from you now. Yes, I have issues, but you said if I am sincere in my request, you will delight in me. I need you to fix me, lead me into a path of righteousness. Restore my soul, and uplift my bowed down head. I know that I've made some bad choices, but I want you to forgive me and make me whole again. I am coming to you with no hidden agenda, nor for material gain. I only want my spirit to line up with truth and holiness. Thank you for giving me this opportunity to come into your presence. Let me be forever changed just by calling on your name. Jesus, Jesus, Jesus, how I love you and choose to serve you and you alone. Fill me up with all those things that are holy, pure, and of good report and satisfy my lips with good things. In Jesus's Name, Amen.

Notes

_____

_____

10
HOW MUCH WILL IT COST?

How much will it cost? This is the question we usually ask when we really want something and need to make a good choice prior to making the purchase. We want to make sure that we can afford it, even before we know the amount. Do you think it would be helpful to know how much that one-night stand was going to cost? That late night creep or those off site hustles, prior to you participating in them. Would it change your decision to purchase that experience?

I must tell you if I knew that sin would have the effects on my mind, body, and soul the way that it has, I would have requested a full refund. It is too costly to play on the enemy's court. He will make you think the game is yours until you are losing and then he sweeps the floor with your dignity. The cost of sin is pricey and you often spend several years paying for something that only lasted a few days, weeks, or months. What were you thinking? Okay, I cannot point the finger because I have been down this road many times. I have spent decades (literally) trying to recover what the devil stole from me during my moments of insanity. It's all good, God is doing the recovering for me now, but that is only because I have yielded to him and allowed him to totally bring deliverance to my soul.

Don't waste any more time, especially after reading this portion of the book on things that will cost a whole lot in the long run. You are worth so much more than that. Many times, we as women will put up with something because we think "it has to change". Well after several years and much heartache, we realize that it never did. Why are we willing to pay the cost for something that should have never been on the shelf? Girl, get your life back and ask God to totally transform your mind. Then, you can have a full refund. I mean it! God will restore your joy, peace, laughter, positive friendships, family, and more. Go ahead, let it go. It's way too expensive.

A Moment to Pray

Lord, on this day, I realize the importance of being committed to serving you. I understand why I cannot compromise what you have placed inside of me trying to fit in with those around me. You have a special purpose and the enemy has tried to keep me distracted with things that are way too pricey. I don't want to miss out on your provisions for me. I want to be faithful and committed from this day forward to the ministry that you have for me.

I know that you desire excellence from me and that is what I will offer unto you. Let my mind be transformed every time I enter your presence. I love you and I will not give up. I will remain focused on being obedient to you, and getting rid of the expensive sin in my life. Thanks for understanding me.

Notes

_____

_____

_____

11
WHICH ONE ARE YOU?

I will go through this section and describe what I believe to be 5 different types of people. As you read this section try to identify yourself, or potentially see yourself as one of these. You are special and you definitely have a place in this world. Which one describes you the most?

THE FRUIT BEARER

When God made you, he knew exactly what to do for He placed everything you would need inside of you. He knew the trials that you would face and even the victories you would win. Your whole purpose on this earth was already defined from the day you were born.

You are an asset to this world, a powerful gift that will move others into their destiny. Your misery will become your ministry, and you will bear much fruit that will feed those that are in need; not physical food, but spiritual food. Continue to walk in the presence of God and lean not to your own understanding for through Him all knowledge, wisdom, and understanding are obtainable. You are the bearer of good fruit.

THE CATALYST

Part of your role on earth is to initiate change in others. You are ambitious and eager to succeed in life. Your passion is being revealed each and every day and you will find yourself becoming more of a mentor to those around you.

You are sophisticated and powerful beyond your realization. Get lost in Him and watch how He will guide your life in a way you only dreamed. God is an awesome deliverer and will keep His hand upon you as long as you allow. Continue to reach out and know that as you give, He will be giving back to you.

THE LIGHT

You are an earth angel, as you walk this earth there will be many that doubt your ability to make things happen. Know this, that you are one of my most precious treasures. You are "the light".

The light erases darkness and brings hope. It restores dark places and remains strong even in the midst of trials. It is a creation of God, just as you are and will continue to be. You have a job to do. As you grow in Him, He will show you exactly what your ultimate purpose is. Continue to let your light shine, because it is your light that will help show others the way.

THE INSPIRATION

You will soar above the clouds and catch everyone's attention as you take flight.

You will pull others along with you and destroy yokes of bitterness, anger, and heaviness. You have a message that will be felt and heard. You will provoke positive thinking amongst those around you.

Move into your season and grab hold to God like never before, this is your grooming season. God will provide you with all the tools you need to make a difference in the lives of others. You are a great inspiration to those around you.

THE TRUTH SEEKER

You are on a continuous search of who you are. You remain close enough to learn and lean, but distant enough not to get hurt. You will find yourself empty many days in your search for the real thing.

God will have to show you in plain terms who he is and what he can do for you. Don't miss the boat while waiting on a ship; God knows what you need and when you need it. Don't waste time playing games. The truth will make you free. Seek the truth, find the truth, breathe the truth, and share the truth. You are the seeker of truth.

"Open up your eyes and you will see, Open up your heart and you will feel, Open up your mind and you will know that which is the good and perfect will of the Lord." Heb. 10:35

A Moment to Pray

This is the day that you have made and I shall rejoice and be glad in it. Your love is so amazing, your protection is so awesome, and your favor does not fail. I feel so honored by your presence and I worship you.

78

With all that I am, and all that I have, I submit to your holy will. You've laid the perfect foundation through your word for me to live a full and prosperous life and I give you glory. You are Jehovah Jireh; you constantly provide for me, you make ways when things seem impossible.

As I enter into your gates with thanksgiving and your courts with praise, receive my worship. I desire you more than anything in this world. Nothing compares to your loving touch, your hand of mercy, and your gift of wholeness. You are the one for me and I am the one for you. Use me Lord, get the glory out of my life. Let the words of my mouth, and the thoughts of my heart always be accepted in your sight, for you are my strength and my deliverer.

Oh God, I worship you, with the fruit of my lips I give you praise. You are holy, and your mercy is endless. King of Kings and Lord of Lords, whatever your desire is, I want to fulfill it. You are my comforter, and my escape from the cares of this world. Hide me, under thy glorious wings and keep me from all evil. You fulfill my deepest desires and I will obey you. I thank you for always looking out for me and calling me in when I've gone in the wrong direction. Thank you for not turning your back on me! I love you and I worship you.

Notes

_____

_____

_____

_____

_____

_____

_____

_____

_____

_____

_____

_____

_____

_____

_____

_____

_____

_____

_____

_____

_____

_____

_____

12
HARMONIOUS RAIN

"Harmony is as refreshing as the dew from Mount Hermon that falls on the mountains of Zion. And the Lord has pronounced his blessing, even life forevermore." Psalm 133:3

This scripture is saying "When you can live in harmony with your brothers and sisters, you please God. I know it is not always easy with the different personalities and attitudes that change on the day-to-day basis. However, if you are really trying to live a life that is pleasing to God, you must learn how to live in harmony with those around you. Now we know that people press their luck a whole lot, and we do, too. During those times we need to ask God for patience and to help us to be positive trendsetters. Where Godly love lives, the enemy cannot destroy. Love and harmony must become your way of life.

The way we can live in harmony and unity is by practicing giving each other space, but also make time to communicate (not argue) about things that may bother you about your sister or brother. Talk about those things without yelling, pushing, and fighting. This goes for our natural brothers and sisters, as well as our spiritual ones. So many times, jealously tries to rear its ugly head in the equation. The thing about jealousy is that it starts with something small and then matures over time, if untreated. Don't give it the ammunition to grow. Things that mature jealousy are: hurtful words, destructive plots, anger, and hate.

I grew up with 6 sisters and 3 brothers, so I know this works. You cannot allow every little thing to bother you and sometimes you have to be the bigger person and walk away. I have not been saved all of my life so we did have some "throw downs", but once I got saved, I realized that I would have to guard my heart and allow God to fight my battles.

The enemy desires to steal, kill, and destroy and many times he uses those closest to us to bring division so that he can steal our joy, kill our spirits, and destroy the plans that God has for our lives. We must be persistent in our walk for unity and strive for perfection within ourselves. I have learned, the more I become like Christ, the least likely I react to the things that challenge my character.

We must continue to pray that God brings unity between you and those you love.   Even if it does not happen right away, know that God hears you and He will do it! Walking harmoniously with your brothers and sisters is a process. Don't allow yourself to give up after your first attempt; just keep trying.

Don't allow the enemy to make you miss out on the wonderful things that are waiting for you. Life is too short to spend it outside of harmony.

Scriptures to read:
Romans 15:4-6
Ephesians 4:3
Colossians 3:13-15

Charity or love begins at home and is spread abroad or outward. Try to treat your loved ones better than you treat those outside of your own home, and watch God move on your behalf. It is great to give to others outside of your own house, but make sure that those around you feel the love first. It is the best witness to your family when you can love them in spite of their flaws and not charge them off so easily.

I've realized that sometimes it's easier to face the outside world with a mask than to be truly authentic, but such is a waste of your purpose. God desires for your light to shine among your family and strangers. Be consistently the YOU God made you to be. This will be key to experiencing the harmonious rain of God.

A Moment to Pray

Lord, I need you to restore the love in my heart for those closest to me. I want to live in harmony with my natural and spiritual brothers and sisters. Lead and guide me as I take this step towards being more like you. For you died for all of us, not just me. Give me more patience, and the ability to forgive those who have hurt me. I don't want anything to make me miss out on your blessings. I release those who have held me spiritually hostage, along with all bitterness and anger. I accept your love in exchange. I am new in you, and with your help I will be who you've called

me to be. I thank you in advance. In Jesus's Name.
Amen.

Notes

_____

_____

_____

_____

_____

_____

_____

_____

_____

_____

_____

_____

_____

_____

_____

_____

_____

_____

_____

_____

_____

13
THE CHANGING OF SEASONS

The awesome thing about God is that he loves progression. We were not designed to stay at a specific level our whole lives. He is a God of growth and maturity and leads you through situations that foster those two components. Just as we go through natural seasons, there are spiritual seasons, as well.

In Ecclesiastes 3, the Bible speaks of there being a time and season for everything under the sun. Many times, we will go through changes and we wonder what those changes are all about.

I will attempt to bring some insight on how the Lord helped me deal and is helping me deal with the change of seasons. As I was getting ready to graduate from high school, I knew that I wanted to be a Doctor of Medicine. I wanted to go away to college and pursue that dream. The Lord sent me to Kentucky State University in Frankfort, KY. After seeking him for many months, I began majoring in

Biology/Pre-med. The curriculum was very challenging and very competitive and I tried to do the best I could do to maintain what I thought was a good grade point average. I struggled through several classes, some I had to repeat and even then I began to doubt if medicine was what I really wanted to do. To get to the point, I finished and graduated with a degree in Biology with hopes of going on to medical school.

As I stated before, it is a very competitive field and unfortunately my good was not good enough for the schools. After going through a horrible drought of sadness and depression, I finally began to explore other options. To my demise, none of those worked either. As I sat in my Frankfort apartment, I began to ask God, "What now, what do you want me to do? I don't have any plans; I don't have any obvious options. Where do you want me to go?"

Contrary to what I knew at the time, my season was about to change. My boyfriend (now my husband, thanks be to God) decided that he would help me chase my dream. He packed me up and I moved to Indianapolis IN. I didn't have a job, nor was I enrolled in school. I just came by faith and believed that whatever was going to happen in my life needed to happen soon. I was able to stay with my friend's parents for one month until I got on my feet. That really helped me because within one month's time, I had a job paying $7.15 even though I had a BS in Biology, a 1-bedroom apartment, and enrolled in IUPUI. Sometimes, God will take you through a season of humility. These seasons are never easy to adapt to, but the benefits at the end are priceless. I was finally on my way to what I thought was my destiny when another bump in the road appeared. I was failing horribly in the program to which I had been admitted. I found myself studying endless hours, working and trying to take care of my home. No matter how much I studied I couldn't achieve a passing grade on any of the exams. I eventually let school go and looked for a better job.

At that moment I began experiencing seasons of loneliness, depression, anger, and guilt. I couldn't understand why everything seemed to be going wrong in my life. I was trying to live for God, and other people I knew who were not living for God seemed to have the "happy life". I became very frustrated. God had to show me that he was doing much more than satisfying my temporary needs; he was developing my character through my hard times.

To encourage you that are reading this book, know that God is doing something bigger in you, and when you feel that your prayers are not being answered don't stop praying, don't stop getting to know him through his word, keep coming into his presence because He is doing something for YOU. I know is not easy, and he never said that it would be; but he will make "all things work together for your good" (Romans 8:28) when you delight in him; meaning serve him with all that you have.

I ended up finding a job through a temporary service at a hospital. The pay was better than my first job, but still minimal considering all of the education I had. I was working as an administrative assistant for one of the physicians in the hospital. They decided to keep me on permanently and after working for 2 years, I got a big break. The doctor that I worked for decided to apply for a grant that would assist me in going back to school. At first, I was leery about it because I had already failed once, I didn't want to fail again and embarrass him and myself. After much encouragement from my loved ones and the physician, we applied and got the grant. I enrolled in the School of Public Health and after three years of working full-time and going to school part-time, I received my Masters of Public Health.   Again, seasons were changing and shifting in my life, and I had no idea. This degree led me to a promotion to do research and eventually a supervisor of a public health program.   God's plans are always better than our own. Through my struggle, I learned that what he had for me to do was much more than become a physical doctor working tight schedules, and having a super busy lifestyle. Although, if that's your calling; do it, and do it well. He wanted me to focus more on becoming a spiritual doctor; one that would meet the needs of hurting men, women, and children speaking life into them. Those years I spent being humbled and taught by God are irreplaceable, he poured into me so much wisdom, and now I am able to pour into others.

We must be ready to go through the seasons and not become weary when things are not going the way we think they should.   When seasons begin to change, be ready to lose friends, family relationships, and other things. These people/things will no longer be necessary for your journey.

Always remember, that God will not take anything from you without giving you something better. Yes, I found myself doubting many times but when God began to speak to me I could no longer doubt the truth. He has all things in his hands and he cares about every area of your life. Remember, what's good for the present may not be good for the future.

God's path becomes more distinct and clearer as we walk in it. With each step forward, we leave the realm of darkness and travel deeper into his light. Seasons change; but one thing that remains is the fact that God loves you and wants the best for you. If you find yourself stagnant or uncomfortable, chances are you are in transition or you need to be transitioning into your new season. Sometimes it is easy to identify what your next move may be and then there are other times when you must rely on God's voice to give you distinct instruction. Whatever your case may be, be prepared for the shifting of your season. When he speaks, be ready to move and walk into your season.

IN HIS HANDS
It's all in your hands I shall not fear, for all that I do and say, you know and hear.

My life continues to unfold in the way you purposed and planned, and as you lead you constantly extend your hand.

You have made me to know wisdom, joy, and peace and in your presence, I will continue to gain my release.

I am above and not beneath, the head and not the tail, for wherever I go I know you'll always be there.

I am waiting patiently for your call and I am committed to surrendering my all.

I am seeking you daily for your constant favor to help me keep my heart will all diligence and to love my neighbor.

Through you all darkness becomes light and every dry place is brought down and saturated just right.

For you are holy and your glory reigns forever, giving hope to the hopeless and making sure all chains of bondage are severed.

For in you I have my being and I am able to take a stand, for great is your faithfulness and awesome is the power in your hands.

A Moment to Pray

Lord, thank you for the changes in seasons. For I know that through trials, you are molding me for the next level. Help me to get everything I need on this level before moving to the next. I want to be able to inspire someone else through his or her difficult moments. Lord, I am so grateful for your mercy and grace; they are truly sufficient.

On tonight, which I thought would be ordinary; your spirit shined through and healed my hurting heart, wandering mind, and doubtful gestures. I'm so overwhelmed by your powerful anointing. I wept tears of sorrow, pain, and victory all at once. I got the total victory over the enemy and Satan is under my feet. Lord you are so worthy and you saw fit to bless me. Thank you for your anointing and the tremendous calling on my life. Thanks for all the wisdom you are placing inside of me. Thank you for the change in seasons.

Notes

14
SILENT RAIN

There are moments in life where you will hear nothing. You will come to a place where it seems that no matter what happens, God is not speaking. I have come to realize that this is a season of growth, as well. God could be waiting on you to move into the things he has previously spoken, or simply giving you time to wait and build your faith, patience, and determination. I can remember several times feeling like God had forgotten about me. As I spoke about earlier during my transitioning season from high school to college and thereafter I did not know what I was supposed to do and God was not talking. I knew then that I would have to begin to step out on the words that were already spoken and believe that he would take care of me. I know it sounds easier said than done and it is; but when you are desperate you don't have any other choice. During those times of silence, you have to rely on your inner strength to get you through. Trust me, if you get too far out of line, God will speak up. I had a sincere desire to fulfill his

97

will, so sincere that I was afraid of messing up. Fear paralyzes you and keeps you from moving forward. It keeps you from making choices and hinders your ability to walk into awesome blessings. You must address all the fears in your life and command them to die so that you can pursue the dreams within. Don't let fear hold you back and change your mind. Go for what you "think" you know, and if you are wrong then God will work that out, too. We serve a merciful God he knows how to correct you and assist you in producing good fruit all at the same time. Don't be afraid during the silent rain because a new you is being birthed.

A Moment to Pray

Father, you are always present, even when I don't hear you. For your word says that you will never leave me, or forsake me. So I take you at your word today and although I feel uneasy in my mind, and my heart I will trust that you are leading me in the path of righteousness for your name sake. Thank you, for your continuous love, even when I'm unlovable. Show me, how to truly rest in your arms, even when you're silent. I will no longer delay my actions, on the things you previously spoke but I will move with urgency. Thank you for not turning your back on me, and securing a place for me in the heavenlies. I love you Lord, and I will do my part; which is to trust in you completely. In Jesus's Name I pray. Amen.

Notes

_____

_____

_____

_____

_____

_____

_____

_____

_____

_____

_____

_____

_____

_____

_____

_____

_____

_____

_____

_____

_____

_____

_____

_____

_____

_____

_____

_____

_____

_____

_____

_____

_____

_____

_____

_____

_____

_____

_____

_____

_____

_____

_____

_____

_____

_____

_____

_____

_____

15
HOPELESSLY DRAWN TO THE RAIN

Where can I go from your presence?

When you have experienced the constant flow of God, it becomes strange when you go through dry seasons. Dry seasons are those that really make you even more desperate for the rain. God allows these seasons; I believe to develop a deeper yearning and another level of seeking to come out of us. The dry seasons also causes us to examine ourselves and the paths that we have chosen to take. During these times, we begin to question if we have made the right choices, are we doing our best, and what will happen next? These seasons are definitely necessary, though painful. When you are in this place, you must encourage yourself to press even more. What happens when wine is left over time? It gets better. What happens when fruit is left on the vine? It gets sweeter. Sometimes God allows these times to mature us and make us better. Go ahead and accept it, you are chosen of God. Although you don't hear his voice in this season, activate the things you have already heard from him and move forward. Everything God allows is useable. Romans 8:28 says "And we know that all things work together for good to them that love God, to them who are the called according to his purpose." Let Him draw you and drench you with the rain.

A Moment to Pray

Lord God, I thank you for this moment to reflect on where I've been and what I've done, but more importantly where I am going. I ask that you forgive me for allowing myself to be stagnant. I know you desire more of me and I recommit myself today to your plan and purpose for my life. I ask that you saturate the grounds of my heart with your word and your spirit so that I may grow in the things of you.

Break up the hardened areas in my life's garden and plow the fields of my mind with your wisdom. I am ready for movement. I accept the challenges that stand before me and join with you again. This is the day that you have made and I choose to rejoice and be glad in it. I will not give up but I will press toward the mark of the high calling which is in you Jesus. Thank you for satisfying my lips with good things and renewing my youth as an eagle. I am now on track for divine purpose. In Jesus Name. Amen.

Notes

_____

_____

_____

_____

_____

_____

_____

_____

_____

_____

_____

_____

_____

_____

_____

_____

_____

_____

_____

_____

_____

_____

16
CONTINUAL RAIN:
THERE'S SO MUCH FURTHER TO GO

After you've been saved a while you pretty much think you know the ropes. You have your routine down pack, Sunday school, church service, Bible study, prayer and so on. You feel as if you've mastered all things and there's really not much to do. Well, news flash there's so much further to go. We have a divine call from our father to save the lost. When you are in a world where 10 year olds are becoming mothers through rape, women are being used and abused, men are being violated by the system, same sex marriages, and much more, you realize that our work is not done. We cannot become content with the world and be confident just because we are saved. We need to spread this good news to everyone God allows our paths to cross. Yes, it's true everyone will not receive God, but our efforts to help them will not go unnoticed. There's still much to learn. There's much to gain from different experiences. As I continue to travel down life's road of endless possibilities, no matter how much I think I already know or how close I get to what I believe my destiny is, there's always so much further to go.

A Moment to Pray

Lord, awaken my senses and allow me to rise to the occasion that you are calling me to fulfill. I am courageous in you, and I can do anything but fail as long as you are my guide. This is a new beginning and I am taking off the many masks that have kept me hidden. I want the world to see the awesome person you have created. More importantly, I want them to know you. Thank you for releasing a sense of security and Godly pride within my spirit now. I am on my way to greatness, and I will not be held back by fear, doubt, shame, or lack of knowledge. I will possess the land that you set aside for me. Thank you for a new day and enabling me to take flight. In Jesus's Name. Amen

"God will put a weight of glory in your life, turn your stress into strength and the pressure of life into power." Dedrick Murphy Sr.

Notes

17
ADVANCING RAIN

There are times in life that you will feel as if the weight of the world is on your shoulders. You will question the very tactics of God. You will even wonder "Why me? Why now? What for?"

These precious, although tough, moments are used to advance you to the next level. No matter what situation life brings to you, God has a way of using them to make you into the one he has called you to be. You may be saying, "What if I don't want advancement?" You make a good point, but if God had something better for me waiting on the other side of my test/trial then I will endure hardship as a good soldier, knowing that the trying of my faith works patience (James 1:3).

Don't be afraid to sacrifice to obtain the blessing. Yes it's hard, yes you will need more energy from God, yes it will take everything within you at times, but go through the advancing rain because on the other side will be a rainbow of glory! For I consider that the sufferings of this present time are not worthy to be compared with the glory that is to be revealed to us (Romans 8:18).

A Moment to Pray

Lord, I acknowledge your goodness. I confess that I am not where I should be, and I surrender now to your process to get me there. I yield my heart, concerns, and any fears into your hands because I know that you care for me and desire for me to prosper. Use me as your instrument; I trust that you know what's best for my life. Even when I grow weary, or uncomfortable help me to maintain a place of determination and endurance. I am yours, before the foundations of the world you knew me, I will make my existence count. I love you and appreciate your patience with me. I am ready In Jesus's Name Amen.

Notes

_____

_____

_____

18

DELIVERING RAIN

Throughout the remainder of this book I would like you to experience what I call delivering rain. The words that are written in each poem express different levels of my faith and my walk with God. At times, I would cry and be totally disappointed in the place I was in and then God would remind me of how precious I was to him, and how much he valued our time together.

These sonnets of my heart brought out the worst and the best in me. When you open yourself up to God, you never know how he will come in and use the very thing you were told you weren't good at; to be the weapon that will destroy the enemy. I am confident, that He that has begun a good work in you will perfect it until the day of Jesus Christ (Philippians 1:6). My prayer is that you will find encouragement in these pages as you stand in the delivering rain.

While on My Knees

While on my knees, I hear the Lord say, "Give to me your life this day".

When I grow weary from my life's journey, I hear the Lord speak, "I am doing a work in you and perfecting your story" When feelings of lack seem to compass round about me, I hear the Lord say, "I will give you what you need and you will have plenty". While on my knees, I can pour out whatever it is that has been keeping me bound, to allow my broken heart and lost soul to be healed and found. When I am there, I feel so much peace and deliverance from sin, just by opening my mouth and praising God from within. While on my knees, I feel seasons in my life begin to change, making room for new things and old things are being rearranged. While on my knees, I feel the power of God like I've never felt before, moving me beyond the veil into Heaven's door. While on my knees, I feel a great release coming on, in the midst of God's power, I am once again made strong. It only took a little time for me to see, that while I am on my knees, God always hears me.

Emotions

During the moments of silence, my thoughts run wild, wondering what will happen tomorrow. I feel like a hopeless child.

My heart stretched from north to south and east to west, only God knows what I deserve, and I am sure it's the best.

All twisted and tied up in ropes that I thought were made of love, clinging to my inner most being, fitting tight like a glove.

Which way is up or even down, I try to keep on my smiling, but it ends up as a frown.

In the public eye, I show such high self-esteem, but in myself I know I need to be delivered and even redeemed.

If people only knew what was going on inside, they would run for cover and maybe try to hide.

God only knows what my future holds; from day one of my life's story, that's what I've been told.

So I take each day, one step at a time, with these encouraging words playing in my head like a tape on rewind.

"Delight yourself in me and I will give you the desires of your heart, let the love I provide constantly impart words of wisdom, understanding and truth. Let not your heart be troubled while I am doing what is best for you."

With these sweet words whispering in my ears, all I can do is surrender and give Him all my fears.

As time goes by, I'm sure I will find the key to escaping my troubles and leaving all worries behind.

Until then, all I can do is hope and pray, that the life I live reflects God's way.

Even when I feel as if I've done enough, I must keep on going and remain tough.

For in a little while I will see,

Why God intended for this struggle to be upon me.

God's Warmth

As I wrap you in my arms of comfort, I offer you my grace

I'll give you strength to run further and the power to win the race

I have called you out of darkness into my marvelous light,

To give your soul rest and spiritual insight.

There is no limit to what I am able to do

For my grace is sufficient and my favor is upon you.

So lay in my arms, as I hold you close
Because with me by your side, you will always have
the best and the most.

FLY

I see a beautiful angel with huge wings, white as
snow, and then I see this little girl with her head
bowed down and tears streaming down her cheeks.
The angel is looking at the little girl trying to figure
out the best way to dry the tears from her eyes, and
as she waves one wing the girl looks up, she waves
the other wing and the girl begins to dry her eyes,
she waves both wings and the girl begins to stand
up. The girl suddenly feels an overwhelming
strength, power, wisdom, and understanding. It
suddenly feels as if she is walking on air. She looks
down and she no longer sees her feet, but she sees
the angel's wings carrying her. That little girl is you...I
see the spirit of God watching you to see what is the
best way I can reveal a deeper sense of my love to
her? How can I show her I desire to see her
prosper? How can I prove to her just how special she
is to me?

117

I know that you may realize that for every level of Glory you must be given a new Story...a testimony to exclaim victory over the devils trap. God has your destiny in the palm of His hands and your angel is watching closely to make sure that the plan He has for you comes to pass. So, I said all of that to say this, "FLY".

F eel the
L ifting of
Y our Angel

With tears in my eyes I proclaim on this day that you FLY. Despite what people may say or do to try and harm you...FLY...When those you love and trust turn their backs on you... FLY...Because it's when you FLY... your worries, fears, and doubts all seem to drift away.

Waiting

I must wait on the Lord in everything I do.
I must prove to Him that I trust Him and His timing for my life. Waiting is an act of faith and a lying down of self-will.
I must wait and not faint.

They that wait upon the Lord shall renew their strength; they shall mount up on wings as eagles; they shall run and not be weary; and they shall walk and not faint. Isaiah 40:31

Learn Love

Sometimes it's hard to love someone else when you don't even love yourself. You're constantly trying to improve on your love for another, all the while working to no avail because you don't know what it means to be loved. How can you give something that you don't possess? Love is a win, win situation, and with it you are able to overcome and conquer the world. I am persuaded that nothing shall separate me from the love of Christ, not depth, nor height, nor things present nor things to come………my heart belongs to God and with him I am able to do great things. I have strayed long enough, but now it's time to forgive and be forgiven, time be healed in order to heal others. I dedicate this vessel unto you, no matter how many times it takes for me to give myself to you until your work is complete I will keep coming back, and even then I will long to be in your presence.

Oh Lord

I long for thee Oh Lord in the middle of the night
To rescue my soul, and get the devil out of my sight

I long for thee Oh Lord every minute and every hour
To cradle me in your arms and surround me in your
"safe tower"

Oh Lord Oh Lord how I call on thee
To deliver my soul, please don't let me just be

Oh Lord Oh Lord I call on your name
Please don't allow your child to be put to shame

Oh Lord Oh Lord you've constantly been faithful and
true
Save my soul from destruction and allow me to seek
you

My soul is empty and I need to be filled
With your peace, joy, and love let me now be healed

Soulful Praise

The power of praise springs forth from my lips, thrusting me into his presence and causing me to bow down my hips
To totally submit to the Holy one and give Him reverence for who He is and what He has done
My voice sings words full of adoration and honor surrendering unto you a more Soulful Praise, while lifting my heart and with my hands raised
It is not just because I feel your soft and gentle touch, but I cannot help but to notice how you love me so much
Draw me nearer to your precious throne and never leave me comfortless or alone
For this is the hour that my soul cries unto you for total praise is what you are due
No more traditional praise will I give unto Thee, for You have proven Yourself over and over again to be much more than awesome to me
So when I stand in awe of you and your splendor, a more soulful praise is what I will surrender

Tears

Unleashed emotions that express the way we feel
A broken heart or a wounded soul, tears can begin to
heal

Taken by much grief, sorrow, or great joy,
Tears only serve to help not to destroy

Can a man cry and still be strong?
Even Jesus wept, and He never did any wrong

This expression of emotions only work to serve you
Proving it to be a method of development and a time
of renewal, too

Cast your cares upon the Lord for in Him there is
hope
He'll give you strength to wipe the tears and the
ability to cope

Everything we go through happens for a reason
We could be reaping what was sown or it could just
be testing season

Stand on God's promises and know He is faithful and
pure
For only He knows the remedy for your life and your
soul's perfect cure

Take refuge in His love and peace in His grace
For we could not have made it this far if He had not
ran the race

Hold on just a little while longer and don't you even
sway;
Because God has given us the tears that we cry to
help us see the way.

The Light

God has given you a light you must not let it die. If
you are feeling hurt, hindered, or discouraged, just
look to the sky.
When dark clouds come out and look as if they will
stay, look deep within yourself and let your LIGHT
show you the way.
God has called you out of darkness into
HIS marvelous light. He has given you the ability to
stand and the power to fight.

So, let your lights continue to shine, and with God's grace and mercy He will help you endure all the hard times.

When Will I Know

Give me a dream and I will walk it out.
Give me praise and I will sing and shout.

Show me the good that shall someday reign.
Show me how to let my light shine and allow victory to be proclaimed.

How long must I go without knowing my whole story?
How long will it be until I see your infinite glory?

When will I discover all that I am to be?
The result of living holy to reach eternity.

I am tired of a world tied up in sin.
My eyes have seen enough wrong, I don't want to travel those roads again.

My heart is overwhelmed and I feeling worse than down.

Please tell me the essence of my story and the
motivation for gaining a crown.

I empty out myself to only be filled by you.
Please hear my cry O' Lord and tell me what to do.

Why I Love

I knew it was love right from the start;
The way you took joy, love and peace and placed
them in my heart

I can never repay you for what you've done,
The Great I am, the Holy One

For seasons may change and people will come and go
But you are eternal and you always let us know

That no matter how bad we mess up or dig a deep
hole,
It's your desire to heal and save our souls

As I wait on your sweet and gentle touch,
I'm constantly reminded of why I love you so much

Was it the fancy car, beautiful home, or dainty
clothes and shoes?
No, none of the above do I believe you would use
For before the world was formed you knew who you
would choose

To carry the blood stained banner near and far
God almighty, Lord of everything that's who you are

You never skip a beat you just keep on going,
Watching every step we take and every seed we've
been sowing

You let us know when we are on the right track
And if we are not, You make us take a step back

Only to begin all over again, brand new
So that the work you've purposed for us we can
continue to do,

So Lord, I give you praise for being so faithful and
true
You've proven yourself over and over again and
that's why I Love YOU

Keep your heart with all diligence, for out of it spring the issues of life. —Proverbs 4:23

Personal Reflection

"I AM NOT THE ONE"
I am not the one you can pick up today and put down tomorrow. I am not the one that you can walk on like a dirty old mat. I am not the one that you can change like a pair of shoes, I AM NOT THE ONE. I am worth more than money, a one-night stand, a secret rendezvous, or a midnight creep. I am not the one who will remain in the shadows. I AM GOLDEN, I AM PRECIOUS, AND I AM PRICELESS! I am not the one who will settle for what was never mine, nor will I wait for things/people to make things happen for me. I AM A CHAMPION, I AM NOT THE ONE. I am resilient, I am the legacy of blood sweat and tears and I will not give up. Women, Men, Young boys and girls be the STANDARD! - Not the one who shrinks back. A new day brings new choices, Choose NOT TO BE THAT ONE.

A Heart Thirsty For Him

Oh, Lord I lean not to my own understanding. My only desire is to love and trust you even more. With the world in chaos all around me, I find comfort and peace in knowing you. You are my strength and shelter my very help in trouble. Balance me so that, I do not worry and do not fret. Guide me so that I do not err for lack of knowledge, and hide me from the weapons of my enemies. I'm thankful for your grace for it carries me, I'm thankful for your mercy for it protects me and I'm thankful for your favor for it precedes me. Let my mind be renewed in your presence and my heart be filled with your glory. Visit me, hold me, love on me, pamper me, wash me, and shower me. I am yours and you are mine, keep me in the center of your will. My heart pants after thee, I'm so thirsty for you. Go beyond my words and see my heart, go deep within the very essence of my soul to see what you've created in me. I am you, a gentle reflection of your undying mercy. See me, Touch Me, Handle Me. I wait in amazement of your visitation. Courageous King, Magnificent Maker of ALL, how I love thee there will never be enough words to describe what you mean to me.

When Heaven Calls Our Name

When Heaven Calls our Name where will we be? Will there be any others around to see?

When Heaven Calls our Name what will be the sound; that encompasses our being and separates us from the world around.

When Heaven calls our Name what will be left undone? Will it be before we can raise our daughters and our sons?

When Heaven calls our Name all worries will be over as we move to the other side, with our hands lifted up and Jesus as our guide.

When Heaven calls our Name our life's work will be finished, no more checklist, no more storehouses to replenish

When Heaven calls our Name, it will be the sweetest melody. For on we will go from this life to live eternally. When Heaven calls our name.

Dedicated to my mom-in-love. (Helen Jean Murphy "aka Granny Gee Gee") Rest on Momma

Endure & Press

When the trials of life begin to encompass you, remember these two words and the God of our salvation will give you what you need to make it through. He will never leave you comfortless so when in doubt refer to these two refreshing words Endure and Press.

E arnestly seek God's face

N ever give up on His promise

D o whatever it takes to prepare you for the ministry

U nderstand that the trying of your faith works patience

R each forward and forget those things, which are behind you (that includes yesterday it's finished)

E nter His gates with Thanksgiving and His courts with Praise

&

P ut on the whole armor of God so that you are able to withstand the wiles of the devil

R eal Holiness begins within.... feed your soul with the word of God

E nlighten your mind with the wisdom that God imparts

Set yourself in a place to receive his divine direction

Sanctify your vessel (make it a vessel unto honor)

My prayer is that you've been blessed as I've shared some of the precious moments I've had with our Father. That's right, he belongs to us and whatever you are expecting him to do, don't waiver.

God desires to restore and give you an expected end. His thoughts towards you are good. May you continue seeking his face through time in the word, prayer, and meditation. He's a good Father and only wants to see you walking in divine purpose and encouraging others to do the same. I pray that you're able to quiet the noise of your busy life and allow our Father to drench your soul with spiritual rain.

Notes

_____

_____

_____

_____

_____

_____

_____

_____

_____

_____

ABOUT THE AUTHOR

Jennifer was born to Archie and Joyce Shurn in South Bend Indiana. Her parents provided a safe Christian home environment to help her grow and thrive. She has 9 siblings (6 sisters and 3 brothers) whom she loves and enjoys spending time. Jennifer began her relationship with God at 12 years of age; although not perfect, she strived to make her life one of purpose. After high school, she began her college career at Kentucky State University, a Historically Black College and University in Frankfort KY where she was named and featured in Ebony Magazine as Miss Kentucky State University in 1998. After completing her Bachelor's degree In Biology at Kentucky State University, she moved back to Indiana where she obtained her Masters of Public Health degree with a concentration in Behavioral Health at Indiana University Purdue University at Indianapolis. She has spent the majority of her professional years serving pregnant and parenting women in various roles through the Marion County Public Health Department. In 2007, she married Dedrick O. Murphy Sr. and began an exciting journey. In 2009, she and her husband co-founded a not-for-profit called

Murphy Mentoring Group, Inc. The community-based social service organization provides life and social skill development to children, youth, and families in Marion and surrounding counties and in the northern part of Indiana. Her biggest accolades to date are being a wife and a mother of 3 beautiful daughters (Haley, Hannah, (and Harper due November 2018) and 1 handsome son (Dedrick O. Murphy Jr "DJ"). She is a very passionate individual who enjoys serving her family, friends, and those within her community. She has served in various capacities of ministry and now serves in ministry as an intercessor at Living Water Fellowship Church where she has served many years as a leader on the Early Morning Prayer call. She loves volunteering at her children's schools and giving her children tools to become kingdom-minded. Her life's mission is to empower those who come in contact with her to fulfill their purpose and excel beyond any barriers that may stand in the way. She works hard, and she enjoys liturgical dance, writing, reading, teaching, mentoring, speaking, shopping, and spending time in God's presence and of course eating "good food".